Psalms on ANXIETY and DEPRESSION

GOD'S TOOLBOX FOR MENTAL HEALTH

By Lauren Bassford

D1607538

Truth
Publications

Taking His hand,
helping each other home.

ISBN 10: 1-58427-567-7

ISBN 13: 978-1-58427-567-1

All graphics: istockphotos.com

Truth Publications, Inc.
CEI Bookstore
220 S. Marion St., Athens, AL 35611
855-492-6657
sales@truthpublications.com
www.truthbooks.com

Table of Contents

Preface 5

1. Introduction 7

2. The Physical Effects of Mental Health. 13

3. Answering with Authenticity. 19

4. Psalms and Happy Endings 25

5. Answering with Meditation. 31

6. Psalms and Uncertainty. 37

7. Answering with Repetition 43

8. Psalms, Sin, and Mental Illness 49

9. Answering with Speaking Truth 55

10. Psalms and Hopelessness. 61

11. Psalms and Isolation. 67

12. Answering with Challenges. 74

13. Review. 81

Preface

This workbook is designed to be used for either individual or group study. Each lesson begins with a psalm. Read the psalm in your translation of choice, then use the paraphrase in the lesson to sing the psalm. Remember, the psalms were written to be sung! All paraphrases are used with permission from *Worshipping with the Psalms* by M.W. Bassford.

After reading and singing the psalm, pause a moment to reflect on your intellectual and emotional reaction to the psalm in both its forms. These psalms are designed to have an emotional effect! On the following pages of each lesson you'll find material on the topic of the lesson, as well as questions designed to facilitate further thought and discussion in a group.

The final section of each lesson includes projects. These projects take us out of our fill-in-the-blank comfort zone and challenge us to think broadly about the ways in which the psalms should change our lives. Some of these projects are writing, some are art, some are action.

This book came from months of contemplation of the mental health crisis in America and how it affects those in the church, especially women. I pray that God will use this study to bless you and yours, and that it will make you a more fruitful and fulfilled servant in His kingdom!

Lauren Bassford

Lesson One
Introduction

Read: Psalm 3.

Sing: Psalm 3, to the tune of "The World's Bible."

O Lord, my foes are many;
The wicked prowl abroad,
And many say about me,
"He has no help from God."
But You, a shield about me,
Who lifts my head on high,
Will hear me on Your
    mountain

And answer when I cry.
I woke again at morning,
For You sustain me here.
Though thousands rise
    against me,
Still then I will not fear.
Arise, O Lord, to save me
And shatter all my foes
To You belongs salvation,
So bless us in our woes.

React

What was your reaction to reading the psalm? _____

_____

_____

_____

_____

What was your reaction to singing the psalm? _____

_____

_____

_____

_____

Study

Mental health is a huge topic. To say that the world is experiencing a mental-health crisis is probably an understatement. The Anxiety and Depression Association of America claims that 264 million people worldwide suffer from depression, and many of those suffer from both depression and anxiety. The COVID pandemic didn't help. The World Health Organization suggests that anxiety and depression increased 25% worldwide because of the pandemic and resulting social changes. Anxiety and depression are absolutely a part of the human experience. Being Christians doesn't exempt us from suffering from mental health problems. Those in the Lord's church are just as susceptible to mental illness as anyone in the world.

Frankly, though, to hear teaching on it, you'd think that God's people never suffered from mental illness at all. Usually, the teaching I hear falls into one of two camps. The first, and by far the more prevalent, is that Christians, real Christians, *can't* be depressed. It just isn't possible. So, if you're depressed, it's because you're not really a Christian. You don't have enough faith in God. You're letting Satan into your heart. Christians ought to be the happiest people in the world, and if you're not, you're doing it wrong.

The other end of the spectrum pops up sometimes, too. Occasionally I'll hear Christians talk about how if you're depressed, you just need to take meds and it'll be fine. In this worldview, meds solve all the problems, and there's no work to be done, no lingering effects of depression. Medication for mental illness should be able to cure you on its own, entirely.

Sisters, both of these approaches are bunk! They're garbage. If you have one of these in your head, from someone who's told you that you need to just stop being depressed, know that God's word says nothing of the sort. Part of the purpose of this study is to look at what God's word actually says about things like depression and anxiety. We'll also look at stories of God's people, God's anointed kings and prophets, who struggled mightily with their mental health!

Switch the dialogue around and apply the same arguments to someone who has diabetes, or cancer. Would you ever tell a sister with cancer that she just needs to have more faith, just needs to be happy and let the light of God rule her life? Would you tell her that the cancer is actually where she's let Satan into her heart and her body? I really hope not. If you would say that to a sister in that situation, maybe there are other conversations we need to have first.

Similarly, if you had a sister with diabetes, would you tell her to just take her insulin, then carry on eating an entire cheesecake for supper? Would you tell a friend with high blood pressure to take her meds, then chase them with a shaker full of salt? Of course not! All of us recognize that, whatever physical health problem we're dealing with, there's a balance to be struck. We need pharmaceutical assistance sometimes but needing that assistance doesn't mean the job is done.

To add another dimension to the analogy, would you tell a sister with an arthritic knee that, after medical intervention to fix her knee, she should just figure out how to move right and exercise? Or would you agree with her doctor that, in addition to surgery and willpower, she also needs a physical therapist to teach her how to break old habits that she developed when her body wasn't working right? Similarly, sometimes we need medications, willpower, AND a counselor or therapist to help us break the hold of mental illness in our lives.

In order to explore the topics of anxiety, depression, and mental health, the Psalms are an incredibly useful framework. Our exposure to the Psalms tends to be limited. We know the ones that are culturally popular, like Psalm 23. We know some of the ones quoted in the New Testament, like Psalm 22. We know ones that are worked into hymns, like Psalm 42. Beyond those, though, we might have a few favorites, and then the rest of the book is a mystery.

There are several problems with this approach to the book of Psalms. First of all, we tend to read the Psalms as we like to read the rest of the Bible—close textual reading, picking apart every word in every verse. That's useful, but that's not the end of the usefulness of the Psalms. The Psalms functioned as the inspired hymnal of God's people under the Old Covenant. They're poetry. In fact, they're poetry that's designed to be sung. Most modern Bible layouts capture the poetic nature of the Psalms, by putting them in poetic form, but we rarely sing Psalms as they're intended to be used.

We also miss much of the Psalms when we cherry pick them. When we gravitate to the Psalms that we already know, or that our culture tells us are important, we don't see many of the themes throughout the Psalms. Most of the Psalms are dark. They're full of unhappiness, desperation, loneliness, and anger. Psalms like that don't make for great praise songs. Because of their content, many of the darker psalms are ignored in our hymn repertoire, and that lets us think those emotions don't exist in the Psalms or the Bible, when in fact they're the predominant emotions in the book.

Finally, ignoring most of the Psalms limits our emotional range individually and as a group. It's easy for church to become the home of the stiff upper lip, where the only emotions allowed are happy positive ones. Soon, that outlook extends to our entire lives. If we believe that the only emotions expressed in the Bible are happy positive ones, then we will struggle to express the negative emotions that we experience. A deeper understanding of the Psalms gives us a way to voice the range of emotions we feel. Yes, there are happy emotions in the Psalms, but there are others, too, and learning from Psalms will give us guidelines for expressing those emotions.

In each of these studies, then, we'll look at a psalm, usually a psalm with a darker theme to it. We'll sing a paraphrase of the psalm, read the psalm, and then consider how the themes of that psalm apply to our lives. Finally, each lesson will include a couple of projects that will help us explore the concepts in the psalm and how we can use those concepts to help us manage mental health issues in our lives and the lives of those we love.

Psalms on Anxiety and Depression

Discussion Questions

1. What have you heard said about anxiety, depression, and mental illness in a Bible-study setting? How often have you heard the subject addressed?

   We should be joyful.

2. Rate your familiarity with the book of Psalms. Which ones are you familiar with off the top of your head?

   Psalms 119 Longest
   Psalms 53 The fool says there is no God
   Psalms 23 The Lord is my Shepherd.

3. Song is a well-known memory aid. What Psalms are you familiar with because you sing them? Do you notice common elements in the ones we sing?

   Psalm 23, 121 my help comes from the Lord
   62 My soul waits for God alone
   46 God is our refuge

4. Consider Psalm 3, which we sang and read at the beginning of this lesson. What popular praise song comes from this psalm? If you're unfamiliar with it, watch "Shield about Me" on YouTube. What is the tone of that praise song? What is the tone of the psalm overall? Why is this important?

   Faith of my Father
   Holy Faith

5. Read Philippians 4:6-7. How is this context typically used? Is this a fair application? Why or why not?

   Be anxious in nothing. With prayer & petition present your requests to God.
   We shouldn't worry.
   David worried but he knew God would save him.

Project 1

Start a list here of the Psalms with which you're familiar, your initial impression of them, and a quick 2-5 word summary of each one. As you study through this book, keep coming back to this project and add to it. See how your understanding of the Psalms evolves as you learn more about them!

_____

_____

_____

_____

_____

_____

_____

_____

_____

_____

_____

_____

_____

_____

_____

Project 2

Consider your own experience with mental health. Have you suffered from anxiety or depression? Has a loved one? What is your impression of those diseases? What is included in them in your experience?

_____

_____

_____

_____

_____

_____

_____

_____

_____

_____

_____

_____

_____

_____

_____

Lesson Two
The Physical Effects of Mental Health

Read: Psalm 22.

Sing: Psalm 22, to the tune of "Lamb of God."

My God, my God, I groan to You,
So why have You forsaken me?
I cry by day; You do not hear,
By night, but suffer woefully.
Yet You are throned upon our praise;
Our fathers put their trust in You;
To You they cried and were redeemed;
They trusted, and they found You true.

I am a worm and not a man,
Despised by all the people here;
"Now let the Lord deliver him,"
They shake their heads at me and
    sneer.
Yet You have brought me from the
    womb,
O Lord, my only hope on earth;
Upon Your mercy I was cast,
And You have been my God from birth.

React

What was your reaction to reading the psalm? _____

_____

_____

_____

_____

What was your reaction to singing the psalm? _____

_____

_____

_____

_____

Study

Mental health is easy to pigeonhole: "Mental health is in your head." Well, yes and no. "Mental health is controllable." Well, yes and no. "Mental health is all about your state of mind." Well, yes and no. Mental health is both mental and physical. Our desire to separate these aspects is very much a product of our Western culture. Our body is one thing, our mind is something else, and our emotions are a separate matter altogether. In reality, we are each one being. Contrary to Facebook memes, we are neither a body with a soul, nor a soul inhabiting a body. We are both. We are all. Trying to separate something as complicated as mental health into mind or body or emotion is a fool's errand.

Much research has been done into the connection between mind, body, and feelings. The psychology field of neuroplasticity conducts research into the ways in which we can change our minds—literally. Neuroplasticity is a fairly new idea, but it's the idea behind the concept that you can build a habit by repeating the same action over and over again. Similarly, if you repeat the same thoughts over and over again, you can change your mind.

However, this is about more than just repeating affirmations until you believe them. Neuroplasticity has established that you can actually change the way the neurons in your brain work. You can train your brain to be more or less optimistic, to be more or less paranoid, or to be more or less anxious, and these changes actually create physical changes in the brain. God's design for our body and our brain is truly good and so poorly understood!

There's a lot we can tell about someone's mental health by the way she describes her body. Psalm 22, which we read earlier, is a good example of this, but examples appear throughout the Psalms. Psalm 6 is a great example of talking about mental anguish in terms of physical pain. This isn't just a comparison, though. Depression actually hurts. Anxiety actually hurts. Even colloquially, people talk about distressing news being a gut punch, or someone grieving being broken-hearted.

Psalms on Anxiety and Depression

Does the mental pain produce physical pain, or vice versa? It works both ways. Sometimes the mental pain we're in can produce physical pain. Anxiety can cause heart-rate increases and heart palpitations. Depression can cause body aches and an upset stomach. It works the other direction, too, though, especially when physical pain is chronic. Being in constant pain physically causes mental and emotional distress that can spiral into depression. Anticipating pain because you've felt pain in the past can cause anxiety. The body, mind, and heart are too interconnected for something to affect only one part of us and not the rest!

While the Psalms are rife with mental, emotional, and physical pain, other Bible characters suffer emotionally and physically too. Job's trials in the first two chapters of the book are an incredible look at the interconnectedness of different types of suffering. First Job loses his livelihood, in the form of all of his flocks and herds. Then his children all die. All of them. At once. Then Satan gets a running start again, comes down, and attacks Job's physical health by afflicting him with physical pain from head to toe. Finally, Job starts to lose relationships. His wife tells him to curse God and die, and then his friends come and, after observing quietly for a few days, start asking what he's done to deserve all of this.

Obviously, Satan intends to cause both physical and emotional pain. Loss of livelihood is painful mentally and emotionally, but it will cause physical pain as well. The same goes for the loss of Job's children. Ask anyone who's lost a child whether that loss is confined only to the mind and heart, and they'll quickly assure you it's not. Even the physical pain that Satan inflicts also causes emotional pain. You can feel Job's hopelessness as he sits in the ashes and scrapes himself.

Elijah is another Bible character who suffers from emotional and physical pain. In Elijah's case, though, God directly intervenes with a solution for him. In 1 Kings 19, Elijah is coming off of the emotional high of having shown the power of God in defeating the prophets of Baal at Mount Carmel. What an experience! How sure Elijah must have been of God and His ability to do anything. Instead, though, Elijah comes from the highest of adrenaline highs to the lowest of lows when Jezebel promises to kill him. He takes off running, gets to the wilderness, and asks God to take his life because he is so very alone. He's tired of fighting. He's isolated. He feels like everyone is against him.

God's solution here isn't for Elijah to hop up and keep working, or even for Elijah to just trust God and watch Him work. Elijah laid down to take a nap and, presumably, wait for God to kill him. When he wakes, an angel has come and feeds Elijah a snack. Elijah then naps again, and when he wakes is again fed by the angel. After that, Elijah walks forty days into the wilderness, then continues his conversation with God.

Elijah comes to God with a problem that is obviously mental in nature. Elijah is discouraged, hopeless, and depressed. God's answer and solution for that problem isn't as obviously mental in nature, though. God's solution is utterly physical and simple: Take a nap and have a snack. God responds to Elijah's emotional distress with a physical solution. What a great reminder for us! We can't separate our physical condition from our emotional and mental condition. God made each of us as a whole complete being, and all the parts of us interact with all the other parts of us. God intends for physical self-care to be a part of our emotional well-being, as well!

Beware the word *just* when thinking about mental health. Mental health problems are never *just* in our heads. They're in our heads, and our hearts, and our bodies, and our souls. If the problem is everywhere, the solution will need to be everywhere, as well. Mental health problems are not something you need to *just* get over with positive thinking. It will take positive thinking, sure, but it will also require physical care, emotional retraining, and spiritual nourishment.

Discussion Questions

1. When you read Psalm 22, describe your impression of the physical state of the psalmist. Who else in the Bible used this psalm, and in what context?

2. What connection have you observed between physical and emotional pain? Can you identify times when physical pain has caused emotional pain? What about the other direction?

3. What connections can we make between the different types of suffering Job endured? What help does that give us in applying the book of Job?

4. What does your version of "Take a nap and have a snack" look like? What physical rituals or exercises are nourishing and refreshing for you?

5. What Bible story or personal experience has led you to change your view of the interaction of physical and emotional pain?

Project 1

Brainstorm a list of ways you can physically alleviate the mental and emotional pain you may experience. Think through not only what relaxes you, like bubble baths and pedicures, but what nourishes you, like quiet time with a Bible study and a cup of coffee, or a good meal with friends.

_____

_____

_____

_____

_____

_____

_____

_____

_____

_____

_____

_____

_____

_____

_____

_____

Project 2

Exchange lists with a friend. Based on what's on your friend's list, how can you function as the angel in Elijah's story and bring refreshment to a sister who needs it?

_____

_____

_____

_____

_____

_____

_____

_____

_____

_____

_____

_____

_____

_____

_____

_____

Lesson Three
Answering with Authenticity

Read: Psalm 102.

Sing: Psalm 102, to the tune of "Poor Wayfaring Stranger."

Allow my prayer to come before You;
O Lord, incline your ear to me;
Do not be heedless of my trouble;
Be near and answer faithfully.
My bones have burned as in a furnace;
My heart has withered like the grass;
I drink my tears and feed on ashes,
And like a shadow I will pass.

But You, O Lord, abide forever,
And all will know Your victory,
For You will rise with grace for Zion;
The time has come for all to see.
The kings of earth will praise Your glory;
The nations, know Your name and fear
Because the Lord has founded Zion,
And in her glory will appear.

React

What was your reaction to reading the psalm? _____

_____

_____

_____

_____

What was your reaction to singing the psalm? _____

_____

_____

_____

_____

Study

Just as the Psalms give us insight into what mental health struggles can look like, they can also give us insight into some of the answers. One of the ways we can fight back against our mental health problems is to maintain authenticity in the ways in which we interact with God. Authenticity is something of a buzz word in modern American culture. "Speak your truth! Be your authentic self!" By contrast, the heavily curated lives that we show each other on social media or our pasted-on smiles at Sunday assemblies push us in the opposite direction, toward hiding our true selves, thoughts, and feelings.

This is problematic when it comes to our brethren. God gave us our spiritual family to help us and encourage us when we need it most! If we hide our feelings and thoughts, our troubles and joys, from our sisters, then God's plan doesn't work like He designed it to work.

If that's true, then how much more is it problematic to hide our thoughts and emotions from the God who made us and loves us best? God is our best comforter, our best consoler, and our best friend. Not only do we deny ourselves His comfort and solutions when we hide our authentic selves, but—spoiler alert—He already knows anyway! God knows what we really think and feel long before we tell Him. Authenticity is the only answer!

In the Psalm we started off with, Psalm 102, the psalmist is pitiful. He paints a truly awful picture of himself and his mental state. Every mental and body system is just falling apart, and he is completely open about it. There's no hint of the psalmist telling his friends at church that he's making it or he's doing all right. Instead, he lays it all out.

An uncharitable reading of the psalm almost has me rolling my eyes. Burning bones? Withered heart? Eating ashes? Come on, now! Stop being so dramatic! It can't possibly be that bad! Get over yourself!

Psalms on Anxiety and Depression

Of course, these descriptions are not literally, objectively true. The psalmist is not literally eating ashes. His heart has not literally physically withered within him. However, we've all been in places where we feel like that is true. We've had experiences where we are so distraught that it feels like our bodies are burning up, where we're so upset that food loses its taste.

While it may seem dramatic, there is value in acknowledging our thoughts and feelings. When we are in the middle of a difficult situation, it can be easy for us to diminish and dismiss the sincere thoughts and feelings we have. We can use the situations of others to minimize our own troubles—"Well, at least I don't have it as bad as so-and-so." We can use a longer term perspective to minimize our right-now perspective—"Well, at least eventually it'll all work out, when we all die and go to heaven." We can even use the blessings we have to minimize the pain we feel—"Well, my child died, but at least I have another child."

All of these reassurances may be true. Someone else probably does have it worse. Things will be okay when we're in heaven. You may still have that another child. However, none of those truths erase the truth of the pain that is present at the moment, and it is acceptable to acknowledge that truth and that pain with your sisters and with God.

We looked at Elijah in the last lesson, in his depressive episode after Mt. Carmel. When God asks Elijah why he's there, and what's wrong, Elijah goes on a tirade: "I've done everything I should. I've served You faithfully. Now it's just me, and there's no one else, and I've done everything I can."

This is not actually true. God will tell Elijah later that there are yet 7,000 who haven't bowed a knee to Baal. That is far from alone! However, God doesn't start there. God doesn't smack Elijah and tell him to quit whining. He doesn't roll His eyes at Elijah's dramatics. Instead, He starts by comforting Elijah. He sees to Elijah's physical needs and comforts him with God's presence. He does eventually speak to the truth of Elijah's statement, but that comes once Elijah's pain has been addressed.

Of course, the need to be authentic doesn't negate the commandment to be joyful and speak truth. Sometimes the cultural imperative to speak one's own authentic truth ends up as a license to whine and vent. This isn't godly authenticity.

The problem is that complaining can affect your mind and cause you to see the world more negatively. Philippians 4:8 offers a wonderful framework for positive godly thinking: what is true, lovely, etc? Think about this. Some see this as being at odds with stories like Elijah's where it seems truth takes a momentary back seat to feeling. They insist that Philippians 4:8 means that regardless of what we feel about it, we must always speak the unvarnished truth right out of the gate.

What do we do with this seeming contradiction? How do we validate our emotions while still valuing truth? The key is recognizing the place that feelings have in the bigger scheme of things. It is absolutely true that Elijah felt alone when he complained to God in 1 Kings 19. It was not true that he was alone, but it was true that he felt alone.

In order to balance feelings and truth, part of our authenticity needs to be a recognition that while I feel what I feel, my feelings do not necessarily represent capital-T Truth. My teenage daughter feels like I am not listening to her reasons for wanting to go be with her friends. Her feelings are valid and true, even if the content is not true. It is just as important to confront the truth of her feelings as the truth of the reality. Both are truth.

Psalms on Anxiety and Depression

Discussion Questions

1. Are you tempted to hide your authentic truth from your sisters? What about from God? How do you feel about this temptation?

2. What rationalization do you tend to use to dismiss your pain? What negative effects come from using that rationalization?

3. How can we learn from God's methods of dealing with Elijah to help us comfort our sisters better?

4. Think of a story in the Bible where someone's expression strikes you as authentic. What can you learn from that Bible character?

5. How do you balance thinking on true, lovely things with authentic expression of your mental state?

Project 1

Think back to a time when you felt desperately unhappy. Depict that time artistically. Use colors, shapes, words, whatever makes sense to you, but create a visual image of your feelings. Reflect on how dramatic that seems now, removed from that situation.

_____

_____

_____

_____

_____

_____

_____

_____

_____

_____

_____

_____

Project 2

Write truth. Think of everything that you can that is true and write it. Write about God, about His creation, about His work. Write about yourself, your feelings, and your experiences. Write about what you see and what you know. Think on truth.

_____

_____

_____

_____

_____

_____

_____

_____

_____

_____

_____

_____

Lesson Four
Psalms and Happy Endings

Read: Psalm 69.

Sing: Psalm 69, to the tune of "Let the Lower Lights Be Burning."

Wine with gall, O Lord, they give me,
And they show no sympathy;
When they are at peace, entrap them;
Blind them so they cannot see.
Pour Your indignation on them,
And consume their tents with strife;
As they scorned the one You
    wounded,
Blot them from the book of life!

When You save me, I will praise You,
And my song will please You more
Than the gift another offers,
For You love to hear the poor.
So let earth and heaven praise You;
Let the oceans do the same;
You will give a home in Zion
To the ones who love Your name.

React

What was your reaction to reading the psalm?_____

_____

_____

_____

_____

What was your reaction to singing the psalm? _____

_____

_____

_____

_____

Study

I was born in 1981. I was raised on Disney movies, Star Wars, and Friday night Must See TV sit-coms. In these, the prince gets the princess, and they live happily ever after. The good guys defeat the bad guys, and even the bad guys kinda turn away from their bad, in the end. The family learns an important lesson, everything works out, and everyone's happy together at the end of the 30-minute show. I expect happy endings.

Life sometimes doesn't give us happy endings. Sometimes it does; don't get me wrong. The life of the Christian is filled with contentment, joy, and blessing.

Sometimes things don't work out that way, though. Sometimes you spend your whole life hoping for the baby that never comes. Sometimes you find yourself alone in your 40s, raising two kids, instead of growing old with your husband. Sometimes you learn too early that death comes for all of us when you lose a parent young. We expect happy endings, but we don't always get them, and sometimes we don't know what to do with the sad ending and how to process that and still live a life of joy.

Psalm 69, which we looked through at the beginning of this lesson, presents exactly this problem for us to consider. David cries out for God's rescue, details his problems and concerns, prays imprecation over his enemies, and praises God at the end. . . but does he get resolution to his problems? Do David's enemies eventually leave him alone? Is he granted victory over them? As he asks for in verses 22-28, are they punished for their evil deeds toward David? Maybe. Eventually, in a sense, as David eventually dies and is rewarded in paradise. But in the context of the psalm?

This is hard for us to swallow. We prefer the Bible stories where it all works out in the end. Even stories like Samson's, where he dies but takes the bad guys out with him, are preferable to this. . . lack of resolution. There are plenty of stories of Bible characters who

Psalms on Anxiety and Depression

never get that resolution, though. Even stories like Jonah, where the bad guys are turned into good guys, have that sense of *unre-solvedness*. Does Jonah ever repent of his anger at God's rescue of the Ninevites? Does Jonah see God's point with the plant? Who knows?!?

Even well-known stories like Abraham's have elements to them that are unresolved. When God initially makes His promises to Abraham in Genesis 12:1-3, God promises big. There are some sweeping, grandiose promises made.

What of those does Abraham see? He doesn't see the land promise fulfilled— it'll be hundreds of years before that one comes to pass. He doesn't see the great nation promise, either. That one will start in Egypt, long after Abraham's death. Abraham sees God blessing those who bless him and cursing those who curse Him, at least in a limited sense. That continues on a much greater scale after Abraham's death.

Of course, the biggest promise of all, that through Abraham all the nations of the earth would be blessed, isn't fulfilled till thousands of years after Abraham's death. The writer of Hebrews talks about Abraham's faith being accounted as righteousness—and that has to be true! While Abraham believed God, and was blessed by God in his lifetime, most of the happy ending that God promised to Abraham didn't come for hundreds or thousands of years!

Moses is another Bible character who didn't see his happy ending. Moses tried so hard. He put up with the Israelites for forty years in the wilderness, grumbling, complaining, and trying to stage coups and take over. He asked God multiple times not to just kill the Israelites outright when God was angry and would have been justified in so doing. And yet, Moses didn't regard God as holy in Numbers 20:12.

Moses's disbelief led to some unalterable consequences that kept Moses from his earthly happy ending. For forty years, he'd been leading these people toward the land that God had promised them, evading enemies, refining the faith and behavior of the people, and training them to trust God. However, at the end, according to Deuteronomy 34:1-5, he gets right to the edge, then God takes him. Moses was faithful, but he still didn't see his happy ending.

In a story that hits a little closer to home, Leah saw her happy ending, but also didn't. Leah was the unloved first wife, the hated older sister, who wanted nothing more than for people to love her for who she was. God saw her unhappiness and gave her sons. Read Genesis 29:31-35 and pay attention to the way in which Leah names her sons. "God has seen how sad I am, and gave me a son, so now my husband will love me." Reuben. "God has heard I'm unloved, maybe now he will love me." Simeon. "Maybe three sons will be the magic number." Levi. And then she shifts her attention. "This time, I will praise the Lord." Judah.

Psalms on Anxiety and Depression

Discussion Questions

1. Describe your feelings about the lack of resolution in Psalm 69. Be honest about your reactions. What do we do with that?

2. What Bible story leaves you questioning how it ends? How do you feel about the ending? How do you imagine it ended? What does your imagination tell you about your need for happy endings?

3. What does it mean to you that Abraham believed God, despite not seeing the fulfillment of most of God's promises?

4. Is there a sense in which Moses's punishment seems unfair and seems not to fit the crime? What do we learn from Moses about God's faithfulness?

5. Do you have a Reuben, Simeon, Levi situation in your life? What would your Judah look like? What do we learn from Leah about resting in God's approval?

Project 1

Choose a Bible character who doesn't see his or her happy ending. Write that person's story in your own words. How does it feel? Now, add the happy ending that you know will come to the person—the eternal happy ending. Reflect on the changes made by adding the eternal perspective.

_____

_____

_____

_____

_____

_____

_____

_____

_____

_____

_____

_____

_____

Project 2

Read Revelation 21 and consider the happy ending that waits for us. Find some way to depict that scene—with words, drawings, pictures, colors, whatever appeals to you. Use your creation to remind yourself of the happy ending that's coming!

_____

_____

_____

_____

_____

_____

_____

_____

_____

_____

_____

_____

_____

Lesson Five
Answering with Meditation

Read: Psalm 143.

Sing: Psalm 143, to the tune of "Take My Life, and Let It Be."

Listen to my prayer, O Lord;
Answer as You know is right;
Do not come to judge Your own;
None are righteous in Your sight.

Enemies oppress my soul;
To the ground, they crush my life;
In the dark they make me dwell,
And my heart is filled with strife.

I recall the days of old
And the power of Your hand;
I stretch out my arms to You,
Longing like a thirsty land.

Answer, or my life will fail;
In the morning show Your face,
For to You I lift my soul;
Save me, Lord, my hiding place.

Lead my feet on level ground,
And revive my soul from woe;
Show Your righteousness to me;
In Your love, cut off my foe.

React

What was your reaction to reading the psalm? _____

_____

_____

_____

_____

What was your reaction to singing the psalm? _____

_____

_____

_____

_____

Study

When I was in graduate school, working to become a social worker, I ended up in several classes that involved meditation. I was skeptical, to say the least. We had already had multiple conversations in my classes about whether a Christian could be a social worker at all, as liberal a profession as it tends to be. Now, though, I was being asked to. . . what? Fold myself up like a pretzel and mutter the sacred syllable? I'll pass, thanks. I'll sit and read my Bible because that's what we do.

Then I tried it. At first, it was really okay. I worked at inserting Bible into the exercises I was given. That worked pretty well, actually. Mantra meditation, for instance, can be adapted easily using a Bible verse rather than a secular mantra.

One day, though, we were assigned a guided-imagery meditation. This is where the meditation guide describes an image or a scene in such detail that you can immerse yourself and feel as though you are there. It was a cold snowy day in northern Illinois, and my back was aching, so I did a beach-themed pain-relief meditation. The voice leading the meditation told me to feel the warmth of the sun on my back. . . and I did. I glanced out the window. . . nope, still snowing. My mind had convinced my body that it felt warm sun.

God has created the human mind to be capable of so much more than we realize. Things like psychosomatic illness are a recognized fact. These occur when your brain convinces your body you are sick, whether feeling queasy after hearing of a stomach bug, or being told you've been exposed to strep throat and immediately developing a sore throat.

Our culture likes to deny the connection between mind and body, though. Especially in religious circles, there is a kind of dualism that disconnects the two parts of who we are. There's a quote floating around on the internet, often incorrectly attributed to C.S.

Lewis, that says something to the effect that you are not a body with a soul, you are a soul with a body.

Frankly, those are both incorrect. You are a body. You are a soul. You are an eternal spirit. You are an image-bearer of God. Just as much as God made your soul, your spirit, your personality, your heart, He also made your body. He formed your body to be an integral part of who you are. To insist otherwise is to demean the creative work of God.

As much as we talk about the importance of taking care of our minds and our spirits, then, it's important to also consider the connection that our bodies have to the rest of us. This self-care aspect, though, doesn't necessarily look like our culture's version of it.

As we considered in lesson 2, self-care is more than just pedicures and bubble baths. One important aspect of self-care is Biblical meditation, especially mindfulness. Mindfulness meditation is meditation that focuses on awareness of the body and the breath, as a way of making you present in the moment. When you focus your attention on your body and your breath, you can't be thinking about tomorrow, or yesterday, or what you'll do later, or what you messed up yesterday. You can't think about whether you'll get your happy ending, or what you should have done differently before. You are here, now, in this moment, with God.

The Psalm we started this lesson with, Psalm 143, is a great example of using meditation to be centered on God. David is chased by his enemies, feeling crushed and abandoned. It's so easy, in situations like that, to focus our attention on the problem in front of us. Okay, my enemies have it in for me. What will I do? How can I avoid them? What could I have done to avoid this? What should my next step be? That's not David's solution at all, though. In verses 5 and 6, he tells of his solution: He meditates on God. He remembers all the works that God has done and focuses on those.

What a perspective-shifter!! Instead of focusing on the enemy, David focuses on God. Instead of focusing on what the enemy is doing, David focuses on what God has done. Instead of anticipating the enemy's next move, David looks forward to God's deliverance. Instead of fretting over what the future will bring, David awaits God's mighty hand coming to his rescue.

Of course, that isn't a cure-all. David still has to do something in the moment. However, by focusing on God and His work, David shifts his perspective on the situation. We can do this, too. Meditating on God and His promises doesn't change the difficult situation we're in. However, what it can do is remind us of the relative power of the situation as compared to our God.

Meditation doesn't have to look like one particular thing. The picture in your head when you say meditation is one way to do it, certainly, but there are lots of ways to meditate. You could do a mantra meditation on a particular Bible verse, repeating it and pondering it. You could do a body awareness or breathing awareness exercise. I've done walking meditation, and while it drove me crazy, there are those who love it! Even activities like coloring or needlework can be meditative. I know a sister who quilts, and when she's creating a quilt for someone, she prays for them the entire time she's quilting. That's meditation!

I suspect that even our Lord meditated. In Mark 1:35-37, Jesus goes to pray by Himself. The Scripture doesn't tell us how long He's gone, but by the reaction of the disciples, it's a while. I don't know about you, but I've tried to pray for extended periods of time before. Keeping up a monologue like that is HARD for any length of time. Prayer doesn't have to be a continual monologue, though. Rather than thinking of prayer as a one-sided conversation with God, part of our prayer time can be spent in meditation on God, on His power, occasionally telling Him how wonderful He is and praising Him for His works

Discussion Questions

1. What is your overall impression of meditation? Is it positive or negative?

2. If you were going to remember, as David did in Psalm 143, what remembrances would center you back on God?

3. Read Psalm 119:15, 23, 27, 48, 78, 97, 99, and 148. What biblical concept is discussed here? What do we do with that?

4. Brainstorm some ways you could incorporate meditation into your life. What might it look like for you?

5. When you think of Jesus praying and meditating, what do you think that looked like? Why do you think that?

Project 1

Think of a time that was difficult for you—a time when you felt oppressed by a situation or by an enemy. Write down some of the thoughts and emotions of that time. Next to each of them, consider how centering on God changes your perspective and write your new thoughts and emotions. Then, read each list aloud, and see what emotions each list brings out in you.

_____

_____

_____

_____

_____

_____

_____

_____

_____

_____

_____

_____

Project 2

Meditate! Find a meditation online and try it. If you have no idea where to start, try going to YouTube and searching for "mindfulness meditation" or "guided imagery meditation." It doesn't have to be long but give it a shot. Reflect on your experience and share with the rest of your group.

_____

_____

_____

_____

_____

_____

_____

_____

_____

_____

_____

_____

_____

Lesson Six
Psalms and Uncertainty

Read: Psalm 13.

Sing: Psalm 13, to the tune of "Just as I Am."

How long, O Lord, will You forget?
How long will You dismiss my plea?
How long will sorrow fill my heart?
How long will foes yet trouble me?

Consider, Lord, and answer me;
Reveal Your light, or I will die;
Then they will glory in my end
And mock me with a joyful cry.

But I have trusted in Your love,
And with my heart I will rejoice;
Because the Lord has rescued me,
In gladness I will lift my voice.

React

What was your reaction to reading the psalm? _____

_____

_____

_____

_____

What was your reaction to singing the psalm? _____

_____

_____

_____

_____

Study

I've never been good with waiting. I was always one of those kids who snooped in her parents' closet, trying to find gifts before it was time to open them. I ruined many a birthday surprise by spying out the gift well ahead of time!

As an adult, that turned into an inability to keep surprises secret, too. I can't shop for my friends too far ahead of the celebration, or I'll just have to tell them what I found for them as soon as I find it. That discomfort with waiting bred true in my daughter. After a shopping trip with a family friend, she came home and asked me when Mother's Day was. When I told her it was still about a month off, she thought for a moment, then dashed to her room. She came trotting back carrying a bag, which she presented with a flourish and said, "Happy early Mother's Day, Mom!!" She was so proud of her surprise that she just couldn't sit on it any longer.

Of course, that enthusiasm assumes that the surprise will be a good one. My daughter lives a charmed life for the most part, and her excitement is sweet and contagious. Sometimes, though, waiting for the surprise at the end means waiting for suffering to come to an end. In the psalm we examined at the beginning of the lesson, David asks the same question my daughter did: how long? David isn't excited about an upcoming holiday, though. David asks how long until his misery is ended.

It's a short psalm. It's one for which we don't have much context. We don't know which particular misery David wants to see ended. He just seems weary, though, doesn't he? In some psalms, we see the psalmist begging God for release, begging God to do specific things. Not Psalm 13, though. David just asks, "How long?"

That's a question a lot of us aren't comfortable with. We feel like we shouldn't ask that question of God. Especially when we hear someone else ask it, we respond with tsks. "Patience is a virtue!" is a frequent reply. I think a lot of women of God feel it is inappropriate to question God at all. We'll cover this topic in a later lesson.

Psalms on Anxiety and Depression

However, when the question is, "How long?" it feels extra inappropriate. What difference does it make how long it lasts? It'll take as long as it takes, as my father used to tell me on road trips. Does knowing make a difference?

What's really underneath David's question in Psalm 13 isn't a desire for an hour-and-minute answer. What David is really asking is whether God remembers that he's still waiting. That's obvious in the rest of the psalm. David asks how long God will continue hiding His face. He anticipates that if God doesn't rescue him soon, this will kill him. The waiting is hard, but the uncertainty is harder.

Is this just how life is now? Is this what's going to kill me? Is God ever going to make this stop, or is this my new normal?

God promised children to Abraham. When that promise was made, Abram was seventy-five years old (Gen. 12:1-4). Sarai was ten years younger (Gen. 17:17), so she was sixty-five when the promise was made. Eleven years later, when Sarai is seventy-six, she gets tired of waiting, and Abram fathers Ishmael (Gen. 16:16). Reasonable, right? God made this promise eleven whole years ago! What's the wait? Maybe He needs some help making this happen. Another thirteen years after that, when Sarah is eighty-nine (Gen. 17:17-19), she and Abraham are told that the son of promise will come from Sarah. At this point, it's been twenty-four years since the original promise. How long, Lord? Finally, at the age of ninety, Sarah is blessed with a son from the Lord (Gen. 21:5). A twenty-five-year wait.

How do you feel about that wait? Personally, it bothers me. I know, I trust God. I know how the story ends. But, twenty-five years? WHY? Why on earth did Sarah need to wait so very long? All she wanted was a baby! What had she done to deserve twenty-five years of uncertainty and misery? Keep in mind that at this point, Abraham's relationship with God is pretty new. Abraham doesn't have millennia of kept promises to fall back on to help him trust God.

Of course, underlying my unhappiness with Sarah's wait time is the idea that she is due good things. All kinds of people get babies. Why shouldn't Sarah get one? Why is God withholding this good thing from her? Why is He promising her this good thing, then making her wait for it? If it's good, and she wants it, and He will give it to her, why doesn't He just give it now?

That's my entitlement getting upset at the waiting time for Sarah. Of course, Sarah has her own answer to my questions. In Genesis 21:6-7, she says that the unexpected blessing of Isaac has brought her joy, and will bring joy to those around her.

Our entitlement and expectations often get in the way of our enjoyment of God's blessings. When we think we deserve this or that particular blessing, waiting for it seems unacceptable. Maybe for some, the expectation of acceptance from others makes them cry out "How long, Lord?" For others, it might be the expectation of good health. Maybe some expect a smooth financial path through the world. Part of the impulse behind "How long, Lord?" is the idea that God has messed up our timeline and not met our expectations.

Of course, God defying our expectations isn't just a female problem. The apostle Paul wrestles with that issue in Philippians 1:18-26. He's not at all sure what's coming next. He'll die at some point. He's not sure if this is that point. He doesn't even know if he wants it to be time yet. He sees benefits to staying alive, and he sees benefits to going to Jesus. He's convinced that whatever comes, God will give him the strength he needs to see it through, but he doesn't even know what that strength will look like!

Have you ever been in a situation like this? "I don't know what's coming, so how can I know how to prepare for what's coming?" That's exactly where Paul was, only his "what's coming" was death now, or death later. I would be frantic.

Even with comparatively minor questions, I'm frantic. What do I do? When do I do it? How do I do it? How do I prioritize? Whether it's dealing with health struggles, cross-country moves, educating my kids, or a host of other questions, I'm in a tizzy. Paul isn't, though. Paul is calm and collected. As he wrestles with this question—"Do I stay or do I go?"—he's cheerfully writing letters from prison to Christians all over the Mediterranean. He prioritizes what is most important and lets God worry about what only He can do.

Psalms on Anxiety and Depression

Discussion Questions

1. How do you do with waiting and uncertainty?

2. How do you react to Sarah's story? What thoughts and emotions do you have? How do you react to your own circumstances of waiting and uncertainty?

3. What expectations are underneath your cries of "How long, Lord?"

4. What do we learn from Paul's treatment of uncertainty in Philippians 1?

5. What are you waiting for right now? How can your study help you as you cry out, how long?

Project 1

Create a timeline of your life. Include some of your "how long?" circumstances. What kind of perspective does this give you on God's timeline?

_____

_____

_____

_____

_____

_____

_____

_____

_____

_____

_____

_____

_____

_____

_____

Project 2

Consider some of your waiting times. Maybe there was a good outcome to your wait, maybe there wasn't. Maybe you're still waiting. Like Sarah, we can find joy in the wait. What blessings have come of your waiting? How can you use your uncertainty to praise God better?

_____

_____

_____

_____

_____

_____

_____

_____

_____

_____

_____

_____

_____

Lesson Seven
Answering with Repetition

Read: Psalm 55.

Sing: Psalm 55, to the tune of "O Master, Let Me Walk with Thee."

The Lord will save me when I call
At evening, morningtime, and noon;
He will redeem my soul in peace
And answer them with judgment soon.

The foe has struck with treachery
And kept the covenant no more;
His oily words were soft and smooth,
But in his heart were swords and war.

Give up your burden to the Lord;
His mercy will sustain the just;
He will not let the wicked live,
And in His goodness I will trust.

React

What was your reaction to reading the psalm? _____

_____

_____

_____

What was your reaction to singing the psalm? _____

_____

_____

_____

_____

Study

Women have a bad rap for being nags. There are countless jokes about the nagging wife asking her husband to do the chore over and over again. Part of that is joking, but of course, every joke has a kernel of truth to it. Women see things that need to be done. It's part of how God made us, part of what makes us keepers at home. When we gently remind, whether it's husbands, kids, friends, or anyone else, that can be interpreted as nagging. Of course, no one wants to be a nag!

That avoidance of nagging is especially true in our relationship with God. I've heard so many women talk about approaching God about a subject that's heavy on their hearts. While they're glad for the opportunity to bring their concerns to the Father, they also worry. Isn't He getting tired of me? Doesn't he hate to hear from me on this AGAIN? Maybe I should just take the hint—I've asked already, and it hasn't happened, so He's just saying no. While this impulse to get off God's back is understandable, it just isn't what we see in the pattern of the Psalms!

My husband has been known to say that there are three potential answers to prayer: Yes, No, and How bad do you want it? That last one comes as a surprise. When our children ask us for the same thing over and over, we get frustrated with them. God shows none of that frustration. Psalm 55, with which we started this lesson, shows the persistence of the psalmist in taking his requests to God. Verse 17 of that psalm has David praying morning, noon, and night.

The issue of persistence and repetition in prayer is a complicated one. On the one hand, we have divinely inspired examples like David in Psalm 55. On the other hand, we have Jesus's instruction not to pray repetitively as the Pharisees do. Those seeming contradictions can leave us unsure as to what to do. Additionally, since it's a statement of Jesus versus a statement of David, the inclination to play it safe and follow Jesus's command to the letter further confounds the problem.

Probably one of the most colorful stories of prayerful repetition is the story of Gideon. In Judges 6:36-40, we find the story of Gideon's response to being approached by a representative from God and told that Gideon will lead God's people to take back their freedom from the other nations. Gideon approaches God and tells Him that he'd like a sign that God really meant what He said. This is something we see on and off throughout the Old Testament. Gideon lays out a very specific sign, and God provides the sign.

After that, though, Gideon comes to God again. His first statement is, "God, don't be mad at me, but...." Let's be honest; that's a fair opener. How many of us would even have the guts to try something like that, much less without the caveat at the beginning? Gideon then asks for another sign, this time the reverse of the original sign. God doesn't strike him dead, doesn't sigh heavily, doesn't yell at him. God just performs the sign again, as Gideon asks.

Gideon shows us that God doesn't mind when we ask again and again. He's not going to hit the smite button or register His divine displeasure in some other way. He gets it. In the words of Psalm 103, He is mindful of our frame.

In Gideon's case, God was making a big ask of Gideon. Gideon wanted to make sure God was really really sure. What's the difference, then, between Gideon asking, and, for example, Moses trying to ascertain God's will about going to talk to Pharaoh?

The most obvious difference is in the heart. Gideon was perfectly willing to do what God asked. He just wanted to make sure he was on the right path! Moses, on the other hand, was perfectly unwilling. His repeated requests weren't to make sure he was doing God's will appropriately; they were to try to get out of doing God's will!

I've heard people discount Gideon's story as an example for us because of Jesus's instruction in Matthew 4:7 about not testing God. In the story of Satan tempting Jesus, one of Jesus's reprimands for Satan is that you should not put God to the test. Satan's temptation there had been a direct quotation of the Bible, so the argument goes that just because something's in the Bible doesn't mean it's okay for us to do. Obviously, Gideon did an okay thing, as God gave him the sign and didn't strike him dead, but if ever we ask God repeatedly, we're putting God to the test.

Of course, the problem with that analysis is that we're defining God's words for Him. We look at behavior like Gideon's and call it testing God, and then apply Matthew 4:7 to that behavior. God gives us more information in other places, like the parable of the persistent widow. If ever there was a parable we're uncomfortable with, this one is it!!

In Luke 18:1-8, Jesus tells the story of a widow who wants justice against her opponent. She goes to the unrighteous judge to ask for this justice. The judge isn't especially interested in giving her justice, but she makes a pest of herself until the judge agrees just to get the widow to leave him alone!

I think mostly we're uncomfortable with this parable because it casts God in the position of the unrighteous judge. Jesus addresses this discomfort—it's a how-much-more-so parable. If even the unrighteous judge gives the persistent what they want, how much more so will our good God?

The more important piece here is the widow, though. She doesn't get discouraged. She doesn't wander off and try to fix it herself. She keeps coming back to the one who has the power to make it right!

Discussion Questions

1. How does persistence in prayer make you feel? Does that change as your persistence continues?

2. How do you resolve the apparent contradiction between Bible characters who repeat prayerful requests and Jesus telling His followers not to be repetitive in prayer?

3. What does the story of Gideon have to teach you about asking God for what you need multiple times?

4. What do we learn from the persistent widow? What behavior should we copy in that story?

5. What are you afraid to ask God for over and over?

Project 1

Lather, rinse, repeat! Choose something to pray for and pray for it at least once a day for the next week. Pray for it more often if you'd like! Maybe it's the salvation of a loved one, or a health condition that bothers you, or the state of the world around you. Knock on God's door with that request, over and over again!

_____

_____

_____

_____

_____

_____

_____

_____

_____

_____

_____

_____

_____

_____

_____

Project 2

Read the throne scene in Revelation 4. Draw a picture of what you think that scene looks like. Note the repetitive language—how often do the living creatures repeat their refrain? Does the repetition make the scene less beautiful?

_____

_____

_____

_____

_____

_____

_____

_____

_____

_____

_____

_____

_____

_____

_____

Lesson Eight
Psalms, Sin, and Mental Illness

Read: Psalm 51.

Sing: Psalm 51, to the tune of "Poor Wayfaring Stranger."

According to Your lovingkindness,
O God, be merciful to me;
In Your great love blot out
    transgression,
And wash me from iniquity.
My sin is constantly before me;
I practiced evil in Your sight,
So when You speak You will be
    blameless,
And when You judge You will be right.

In sin my mother has conceived me,
But You desire Your truth within;
With hyssop cleanse and purify me,
Like snow unstained by any sin.
Relieve the bones that You have
    broken,
And teach me gladness in Your grace;
Blot out the guilt of my offenses,
And from my failings hide Your face.

React

What was your reaction to reading the psalm? _____

_____

_____

_____

_____

What was your reaction to singing the psalm? _____

_____

_____

_____

_____

Study

I've tried to spend a lot of time in this lesson series normal-izing mental health problems. Just like it's not an indictment of your moral character if you end up with diabetes or cancer or kidney failure, so it's not an indictment of your moral character if you struggle with your mental health. Anxiety and depression are rampant in modern culture, for a lot of reasons, and no matter how strong our faith, Christians are not immune to those problems any more than we're immune to physical illness.

But. The witness of the Psalms is that sometimes faith does af-fect our mental health. Psalm 51, with which this lesson started, is a prime example. Many psalms are unclear in their origins. We might know who wrote them, but for most of them, we have no idea of the occasion of their writing. Psalm 51 is not this way. This is a psalm that was written by David after his sin with Bathsheba, his sin against Uriah, and his discussion with the prophet Nathan.

2 Samuel 12:15-18 tells the story of some of the mental-health impacts of this episode on David. Once David acknowledged his sin to Nathan, Nathan told him that one of the effects of David's sinful course was that the child created by his relationship with Bathsheba would die. When the child fell ill, David was inconsol-able. The scriptural record says that David refused to eat, refused to sleep, stayed in sackcloth on the ground pleading with God. Everyone in his life pleaded with him to take care of himself in his sadness, probably encouraging him that it wouldn't help the child any for David to die from not eating, either.

When the child dies after a few days, the servants are nervous. Many versions have the servants asking how David will vex himself when he hears the child is dead. Some, like the ESV, are plainer here, and suggest that David might harm himself when he hears of the child's death. The implication is clear: the servants were wor-ried that David would take his own life when he heard of the child dying.

Of course, that's not what happened. David recognized God's hand in what had happened. Rather than continuing in his drastic

Psalms on Anxiety and Depression

course of action, he changed what was in his power to change and repented of his sins so that, in the words of 2 Samuel 12:23, David might go to the child, since the child wouldn't come back to him.

As David reflects on his experience as he writes Psalm 51, he directly connects his anguish and depression to the sin that preceded it. For instance, in Psalm 51:3-4, David acknowledges his sin, and admits that God is right in judging him in this way, as David's sin was great against God. This means that David is miserable over the death of his child, not just as every parent is who loses a child, but also because David recognizes the righteousness of God's judgment and David's own culpability in the matter.

This is a difficult issue for us. It is absolutely true that mental illness does not necessarily imply a lack of faith or a presence of sin. This is counter to what many religious groups have historically taught. When Jesus heals the man born blind in John 9, the opening question is whether this man sinned or if his parents sinned, because obviously someone sinned to cause something so debilitating. That being said, though, it is also absolutely true that sin can and should cause mental distress! There are times when the mental illness we experience should serve to provoke us to examine our lives for sin, repent of that sin, and beg God for healing.

How, then, do we know whether our own mental illness is due to sin or not? There's not a simple answer. For certain, the answer is not to assess everyone we see with depression and encourage them to repent of the sin that we think must obviously be causing their depression. That sounds more like Job's awful friends than anything else! However, this can provide useful fodder for our own personal meditations. When I am miserable, it's hard to see a way forward. Sometimes, though, the way forward is acknowledging what is in my life that needs to not be in my life, and begging God to rescue me.

Psalm 38 is another useful piece of the puzzle. Psalm 38 doesn't have the same context that Psalm 51 has, but it is clearly written as David suffers after having sinned. In this psalm, David reflects on the awful situation he finds himself in and begs God to save him. Much of David's language in this psalm is physical, which makes the connection between mental and physical suffering that we looked at in earlier lessons.

David draws a very definite connection between his suffering and his sin, though. His reaction isn't to vow to do better and clean up his act. He doesn't make promises about how much change he's going to bring about in his own life. He throws himself instead on God's mercy and says that God is the only one who can save him.

In Acts 13:22, Paul calls David by the descriptor we're all familiar with: a man after God's own heart. I think sometimes that moniker gets blown out of proportion. We conclude, David was a man after God's own heart, so he must have been perfect. Or, David was a man after God's own heart, but we know he sinned with Bathsheba, but that was it. He never sinned otherwise. We may even say, David was a man after God's own heart, so he was always in sync with God, and always had his head on straight and his heart in the right place.

Friends, that's just not so. David was a human as we are, he sinned and was miserable because of it, and was still counted as righteous and a man after God's own heart!

Psalms on Anxiety and Depression

Discussion Questions

1. Does knowing the background of Psalm 51 change the way you see it, read it, or hear it? If so, how? Are you comfortable singing it?

2. What does David's behavior sound like, when his son with Bathsheba was sick? What was the root cause of this behavior?

3. Have you ever suffered mental illness due to your own sin? Did it feel different from other episodes of mental illness? What do you do with this conundrum?

4. How would you react to a friend speaking as David does in Psalm 38? What advice would you give them? Does this match David's course in the Psalm? What do we do with the difference?

5. What do you take away from knowing David's story and mental health struggles, and knowing that he was still a man after God's own heart?

Project 1

Draw a timeline of the course of events in 2 Samuel 12. Use color, pictures, etc., to describe the events and the impacts of those events. How does that story look?

_____

_____

_____

_____

_____

_____

_____

_____

_____

_____

_____

_____

_____

_____

_____

Project 2

What does the New Testament have to say about the mental effects of sin? Search a concordance or Google and see what you find. Make a list of relevant passages to see what picture is created by the New Testament writers.

_____

_____

_____

_____

_____

_____

_____

_____

_____

_____

_____

_____

_____

_____

Lesson Nine
Answering with Speaking Truth

Read: Psalm 86.

Sing: Psalm 86, to the tune of "We Shall Assemble."

O Lord, incline Your ear and answer;
I am afflicted and in need;
Preserve my soul, for I am godly;
Be gracious to Your own, I plead.
Make glad the spirit of Your servant,
For You abound in grace to all;
O Lord, give ear to my petition,
And offer mercy as I call.

I call on You, for You will answer,
And there is no one else like You;
Mankind will come and bow before You
To praise the wondrous works You do.
Teach me the way of truth and goodness,
Where I may walk and not depart;
Grant me the holiness to fear You
And give You thanks with all my heart.

I'll glorify Your name forever;
Your mercy to my soul is great;
The proud have risen up against me,
But You will save me from their hate.
Oh, grant Your power to Your servant
And some good sign that all can see,
That those who hate me may be humbled
And know that You supported me.

React

What was your reaction to reading the psalm? _____

_____

_____

_____

_____

What was your reaction to singing the psalm? _____

_____

_____

_____

_____

Study

Our culture is fascinated with truth... kinda. Authenticity is the word of the day, and people are encouraged to be their authentic selves. In a time when self-identity is more important than biology, everyone is told to speak his or her own truth. The implication is that everyone has her own truth, different from other people's truth, that is valuable and unique and authentic to that person, and there is inherent value in that truth.

In contrast, the Bible speaks of capital-T-Truth. This is truth as God tells it, and there is one Way. There are not multiple truths, and truth does not change as you go through your life and grow and experience. This kind of truth is disfavored in modern Western culture, but it is the keystone of Biblical understanding. This kind of truth is also a huge weapon in fighting anxiety and depression.

Psalm 86, with which we began our study today, is a fantastic example of this kind of Truth. This is a psalm of David, but one for which we don't have a context. We know that David is unhappy, feels like the world is against him, and needs God to rescue him. We don't know why, and we don't know what the remedy is.

What's interesting about this one is that, by the end of the psalm, we still don't know what the remedy is. Some psalms will end with the psalmist recounting what God did to solve the problem: "I called to You, and You answered and smacked down my enemies." This psalm is not that way. Over and over through the psalm, David begs God for rescue.

Interspersed with the requests for rescue are some seeming non sequiturs. David will ask God for help, then say what a great helper God is. He'll ask God to rescue him, then talk about God's love for those who follow Him. He'll ask God to stop his enemies, then praise God for His goodness. The problem is that in the context of the psalm, we don't actually see examples of any of those things. We don't see how, in this particular situation, God is a good helper, or loving to David, or particularly good. David's requests go unanswered through the entirety of the psalm.

David isn't reflecting here on the things that God is doing in his current circumstance. Instead, David is reflecting on the things that God has done in the past, and then things that David knows are true about God.

We tend to be super comfortable with praising God as David does in this psalm. We like to sing about God's lovingkindness and His grace and mercy. We usually sing about these when we see them, though. Someone is rescued from a dire physical illness, and we sing praises about God's love. Someone obeys God's instructions for the forgiveness of their sins, and we praise His mercy and grace.

What about when those things aren't happening, though? What about when the dire physical illness isn't cured but results in death? What about when that stubborn family member keeps refusing to see the truth of God's gospel? Do we praise then?

Psalm 77 is another great example of praising when we don't feel like it. This is a psalm of Asaph this time, but it is similar to Psalm 86 in its content. Asaph is miserable. He feels like God has forsaken him, like God has forgotten and rejected him.

His remedy for this is to remember some of God's great deeds. Specifically, this psalm recounts the exodus of the Israelites and the crossing of the Red Sea, but it could have been any number of stories. The problem is, this recounting of the story doesn't actually solve Asaph's problems. Whatever was going on that caused Asaph to feel the way he did in Psalm 77:1-9 still exists at the end of the psalm!

What has changed, then, by the end of the psalm? Asaph's outlook. Speaking truth about God has changed Asaph's opinion of the problems he finds himself in. They're still bad. He still needs to be rescued from whatever is going on.

However, speaking Truth about God's history, His goodness and love toward His people, changes Asaph's attitude from "God has rejected me and abandoned me" to "God hasn't rescued me YET." That yet is huge. That yet keeps Asaph, and David in Psalm 86, from falling into the pit entirely.

We struggle with similar problems with the beginning of James 1. Nope, sorry, joy is not the emotion that comes to mind when I think of going through trial. Joy is actually the opposite of how I tend to approach trial. Even if I try to count it joy, the joy is typically in the ending of the trial. Finding joy in the trial is counter-intuitive, to say the least.

James offers some strategies that help with putting joy in the right place, and all of them have to do with speaking truth. James reminds them what they know, that testing produces patience. In the moment of the trial, I have never felt like it was producing anything good, much less patience.

However, James reminds me that I know that's what is happening. It's truth-speaking. It's saying, "This is true, regardless of how I feel about it, regardless of whether it looks like it right now." He does the same thing in the next verse, reminding them that the patience forged in trial will produce maturity in them.

Again, this isn't what I feel during a trial. I feel like this trial is going to break me, not make me better. That's why speaking truth is so important. Speak what is true, not just what feels true in the moment.

Discussion Questions

1. Have you ever felt like David feels in Psalm 86? What was your response?

2. When you praise God, what do you praise Him for? Are your praises related to the situation you're in at the time?

3. When do you least feel like praising? What do those circumstances have in common?

4. What situation in your life right now needs a yet? What are you struggling with that you can count on God to rescue you from eventually, even if He hasn't yet? What might that rescue look like?

5. How have you reconciled the difficulty posed in James 1? What does speaking truth add to this problem?

Project 1

Illustrate truth. Read back through Psalm 86 and Psalm 77. What truth is spoken there? Create a word picture for yourself—in whatever way appeals to you—to demonstrate the truths contained there.

Project 2

Write truth! Find Bible truth that speaks to your life, to your soul. Write this truth. Share with your sisters and see if the truth they find speaks to your soul as well. Arm yourself with truth from God!

_____

_____

_____

_____

_____

_____

_____

_____

_____

_____

_____

_____

_____

_____

_____

_____

Lesson Ten

Psalms and Hopelessness

Read: Psalm 79.

Sing: Psalm 79, to the tune of "Rock of Ages"

Lord, the nations now disgrace
And defile Your dwelling place!
See how birds and beasts devour
Those who trusted in Your power,
Dying in Jerusalem
With none left to bury them.

Foes reproach us and deride;
How long will Your rage abide?
Lord, pour out such wrath and shame
Where they do not call Your name,
For they put to death Your own,
And our land is overthrown.

Lord, forget our fathers' sin;
Let Your grace come quickly in.
For Your glory let us live;
For Your own name's sake, forgive.
Lest the nations mock Your might,
Work Your vengeance in our sight.

Listen to the captive's cry;
Save the ones condemned to die.
Curse our neighbors sevenfold
For the slanders they have told
So Your sheep may know Your ways
And forever give You praise.

React

What was your reaction to
reading the psalm? _____

_____

_____

_____

_____

What was your reaction to
singing the psalm? _____

_____

_____

_____

_____

Study

Hopelessness is such a difficult concept for me. I thrive on optimism and looking forward to whatever is coming next, and that means that hopelessness is a painful place for me to stay. It's difficult to watch in others too. Hopelessness is a prime area where we offer platitudes to people around us, because it's so very uncomfortable to stay with them in their hopelessness.

A couple has tried for a decade to have children, and even in the face of that, we tell them to keep their chin up because you never know what's around the corner! A sweet 80-year-old woman is diagnosed with stage 4 cancer, and we determinedly offer our support as she fights and beats this thing. It is incredibly difficult to give up hope on something.

Psalm 79 is a fantastic example of this discomfort with hopelessness. Reading and singing through this one is a conflicted experience. The tone of this psalm is ugly. Asaph pulls no punches describing just how struck down Israel is. The first few verses of the psalm are gory and grotesque. We are supremely uncomfortable with descriptions like this. Typically, we either dismiss ("It can't be all that bad!!") or we deflect ("Well, yes, but look at the other blessings God has given you!"). In either case, sitting with the hopelessness isn't an option.

The psalm gets worse from there, though. Asaph doesn't go to praising God for His salvation and redemption or reminding his listeners what a good God He is. Instead, Asaph leads into an imprecatory section of the psalm. Imprecatory is a word that carries a meaning of cursing with it, and it is often used to describe psalms or prayers that invoke curses on a particular person or group. Well, if we're uncomfortable with the hopelessness at the beginning of the psalm, how much more uncomfortable are we with Asaph asking God to pour out His wrath on the enemies of Israel? This imprecatory psalm is pretty mild, comparatively. Psalm 137 calls blessed those who will dash the enemies' babies against stones.

This is the inspired hymnal of the Israelites. This is the content of the hymns that they were told to sing, that they did sing, congregationally! I don't know about you, but even Psalm 79 seems a bit much to sing in the auditorium on Sunday morning. Maybe we'll sing it right before "Sing and Be Happy." I can't imagine!

Psalm 88 is another great example of hopelessness in the Psalms. It doesn't have an imprecatory element to it, but it has despair in spades. This one has no bright side, no call to action, no suggested remedy at all. There is nothing but darkness and gloom. I've heard people suggest that it would be sinful for New Testament Christians to sing something like Psalm 88 because we're supposed to be a joyful people who find hope in God.

While it is true that we should find joy and hope in God, it's also true that sometimes this life is hopeless. Sometimes we are mired in the consequences of our own sin and can't find a way out. Sometimes a cherished goal is simply unattainable, no matter what we do or how hard we try. Sometimes the outcome we had assumed, because everyone else around us has that outcome, isn't the outcome we get.

As I write this, my husband is fighting a losing battle with ALS, a terminal disease that will take his life sooner rather than later. He's 43. I had assumed we'd grow old together and enjoy grand-children and retirement together. That hope is not one that will be fulfilled.

What do we do with those hopes, then, when they're lost? Elijah's story in 1 Kings 19 smacks of hopelessness. Elijah doesn't come out and tell everyone he's depressed. He doesn't say he's hopeless. He certainly doesn't tell people he's suicidal.

However, I think all of those are reasonable conclusions based on what he does say. He has some extreme negative stimuli to respond to—namely, Jezebel's insistence that she'll kill him within twenty-four hours. He takes off at that statement, taking only a servant with him. When he gets out of town, though, he leaves his servant behind. He's isolating himself, which is a hallmark of depression. He lies down in the middle of nowhere and prays for God to take him. He doesn't harm himself, but he asks God to kill him then lies there and waits for it to happen. Elijah was depressed and hopeless. He wanted to die.

God's response is a great learning ground for us, both in dealing with our own hopelessness, and with the hopelessness of those around us. God doesn't smack him around, physically or verbally. As we looked at in lesson two, the first step of God's response is to give Elijah a nap and a snack. God takes care of his pressing physical needs first. Then God talks Elijah through what's going on, by asking questions and letting Elijah respond. Elijah's responses aren't entirely factually correct, so eventually God corrects that misunderstanding, but first, God reassures Elijah. God comes to Elijah where he is, not in a tornado or an earthquake, but in a whisper. God is there, and He is gentle.

Leah's story in Genesis 29 reminds us of an important conclusion to a discussion of hopelessness. Verse 31 starts with God seeing that Leah was not loved. What an awful way to be remembered in Scripture! It's the absolute truth of her life, though, so God gives her sons. The first son is named "Maybe now my husband will love me." The second is named "I'm still not loved, but maybe this one will fix that." The third is named "Is three sons enough to get my husband's attention?" Leah's hope in bearing children is fixed on the love of her husband. She goes to great lengths to try and catch the attention and love of her husband, but it keeps not working.

What would we tell the Leah in our lives? Keep your chin up, honey! Don't give up hope! He'll come around—you're great! Maybe if you wore a little makeup, maybe did your hair? Perhaps, in this age, it would even go to suggestions that if he can't see what a catch you are, you should find someone who does appreciate you!

Leah has a better perspective, though. Her fourth son is named "This time, I will praise the Lord." She hasn't given up hope, not really. That's what it looks like, but it's not. She recognizes the futility of her hope and pins it on something better. Who knows? Maybe five sons would've been the right number, and Jacob would have opened his eyes to the treasure he had in Leah. Leah is done with waiting, though, and with putting her life on hold. Instead of putting her hopes in earthly happiness and love of a husband, she puts her hope in God, and that hope doesn't ever disappoint.

Discussion Questions

1. Has someone ever voiced hopelessness in a particular situation to you? What was your response to them?

2. How did singing Psalm 79 feel to you? Did you feel like you were doing it wrong? Have you ever experienced hopelessness as is expressed in Psalm 79?

3. What have you hoped for that you didn't get, or won't get? What do you do with that disappointment? What strategies have worked for you?

4. Is it realistic to expect that our walk with Christ will always be rainbows and unicorns, and we'll never face severe disappointment in this life? What do the Psalms give us for those times?

5. Where in your life do you need to change focus to praising the Lord, rather than seeking for the hope of this life?

Project 1

Based on God's interaction with Elijah in 1 Kings 19, draw up a game plan for talking to people who are hopeless. What steps can you take? What do those steps look like?

_____

_____

_____

_____

_____

_____

_____

_____

_____

_____

_____

_____

_____

_____

Project 2

Think through some things you've given up on in life. Any time you give up on hoping in one thing, God is there waiting with good things for you. Meditate on the good that God has brought to you after you gave up hope in something else and put your hope in Him.

_____

_____

_____

_____

_____

_____

_____

_____

_____

_____

_____

_____

_____

Lesson Eleven
Psalms and Isolation

Read: Psalm 86.

Sing: Psalm 86, to the tune of "We Shall Assemble."

O God of my salvation,
I cry by night and day;
Accept my prayer before You;
Incline Your ear, I pray!
My soul is filled with troubles;
My strength and hope have fled;
I fear You will forget me,
Forsaken with the dead.

You sank me deep in darkness,
Accursed beneath the wave;
Deprived of friend and blessing,
I call on You to save.
Will You perform Your wonders
For those within the tomb
And show Your lovingkindness
Throughout that land of gloom?

I cry to You for mercy;
Each dawn I seek Your grace;
Why then do You reject me?
Why do You hide Your face?
Your terrors have destroyed me;
They will not let me be;
You take both friend and lover
And hide them far from me.

React

What was your reaction to reading the psalm? _____

_____

_____

_____

_____

What was your reaction to singing the psalm? _____

_____

_____

_____

_____

_____

Study

Yes, this lesson seems out of order. Our pattern has been to spend a lesson looking at the witness of the Psalms to various aspects of anxiety and depression, then a lesson considering a remedy proposed in the Psalms. However, hopelessness and isolation just go hand in hand. They are two sides of the same coin. They are obviously both related to depression, but less obviously, both are a part of anxiety, as well. In both depression and anxiety, the despair of ever getting out of the rut that you are in can lead you to isolate from the very people and resources that can help you out of that rut.

Isolation is both a cause and an effect of depression and anxiety. People with mental health struggles isolate themselves because of them. They think that it will be easier to cope if they are by themselves. Part of this is the brain not thinking clearly. They become convinced that the people in their lives are better off without them around to drag them down. The problem is, that thinking becomes a vicious cycle that causes anxiety and depression to become worse. When we are alone, mental health problems magnify.

We considered Psalm 88 as it related to hopelessness in the last lesson. The real crux of Psalm 88, though, is isolation and loneliness. The psalmist, who is not David, is clearly in a depressive state. Part of the way we can tell that is from the support network he has around him. He has no one. No friends, no family. Part of the complaint of the psalm is that he feels like God has removed everyone from his life. By the end of the psalm, he says that the only friend he has is darkness. These are the words of a man who feels utterly alone, and these are not words that reflect mental healthiness.

Elijah was certainly guilty of isolation in his depression. As we considered in the last lesson, in his hopelessness, Elijah sends away the one companion that he has in his dark moments. It seems he does this to protect his servant from having to watch his master die at God's hand. Even once Elijah gets past the initial crisis, though, his complaint to God is one of isolation and loneliness. He tells God that he alone is left to worship and respect God, and it's just not right that he should have to go it alone.

Frankly, Elijah is right where Satan wants him. A large part of the reason that isolation plays so heavily into depression and anxiety is because the devil thrives when we think we are alone. If we think we are the only ones who've ever struggled with this or that particular sin, the devil is lying to us, and if we believe him, we're much less likely to seek the help we need with that sin. If we think we're the only ones dedicated to God and worshipping Him, the devil is lying to us, and if we believe him, we're not going to seek out the companionship of like-minded believers. If we think no one in God's family cares about us, that we're outsiders in the divine family, the devil is lying to us, and if we believe him, we're going to further separate ourselves from the very people God put in our lives to accompany us on our journeys.

God's response to Elijah, after Elijah gets all his issues off his chest, is to tell Elijah that while he feels alone, that feeling is far from the truth. God informs him that there are yet 7,000 who are faithful to God. In truth, Elijah probably could not have known this. There was no social media to keep Elijah tuned in to the whole of Israel. Elijah knew what he saw. What he didn't realize was how incomplete his perspective was.

That's so true of us, as well. When we buy into the devil's lie that we're alone, even though that lie might feel true, it's a lie. It's not true at all, and the first step to escaping the lie is to recognize it for what it is.

At the same time, though, rebuking Elijah's mistaken belief is not God's first priority. What is the first thing God does in the face of Elijah's isolation and hopelessness? Gives him a nap and a snack. God takes care of his physical needs, then God asks Elijah what's wrong. This pushes Elijah to put his feelings into words.

This is such a huge part of the process of dealing with mental illness. When we get stuck in unhealthy thoughts, they tend to swirl and muddle and get messy. We get to a point where nothing makes sense because our thoughts just stop working well. Forcing ourselves to put order to the thoughts, put words to them, and put those words out where they can be analyzed and assessed is an important step in reframing those thoughts to be useful.

God then shows His presence to Elijah. The wording of this section is fascinating. God prepares Elijah by telling him that His presence is coming. After that, there's a tornado, an earthquake, and a fire. God has shown His presence in all of these things at other times, but the text says that God was not in any of them this time. This time, what Elijah needed was God's presence as a friendly companion, a soft whisper.

Then God asks him again what's going on. Elijah responds in the same way. This time, God addresses the truth claim—there are still 7,000 faithful to God—and sets Elijah on a mission.

The first step of Elijah's new mission, though? God sends him to find a companion. God recognizes the detrimental effect of Elijah's isolation and fixes it by sending Elijah to train his protegee, Elisha. There are other jobs to do – anointing various kings, etc., but Elijah will do them with someone else.

God doesn't just tell Elijah he's not alone, then send him on his way. God makes sure Elijah feels that he's not alone by making sure he has a companion immediately. This is huge. God's reaction to Elijah's isolation is to end it.

Paul is a really interesting New Testament example of the effects of isolation. We tend to think of Paul as Super Christian. The normal rules don't apply to him. This guy got stoned and left for dead, and then hopped up and headed to the next town! Surely, he knew that the presence of God was with him, and he didn't feel the need for silly things like human companions!

That's not the story that 2 Timothy 4:9-18 tells, though. Paul starts off by asking Timothy to join him, and quickly. He rattles off a list of all those who have left him for various reasons, like Demas, Crescens, and Titus. He says that at that moment, the only one with him is Luke. He also asks Timothy to bring Mark with him. Paul talks about the harm done by Alexander, and how he was absolutely

abandoned after giving a defense of his faith publicly. He specifically says that the only one left to him was God, and that God sus-
tained him through that time.

See, there's that Super Christian coming through again. Paul
was utterly alone except for God, and he was fine with that! Except
Paul knew that wasn't sustainable. Paul knew it wasn't good for
him to be by himself. Rather than giving in to the anguish of being alone, though, he does something about it. You can hear his
unhappiness in the way he talks about those who have left. Even in
the way he talks about those who abandoned him, he tells Timothy
that he wants God to forgive them of that, but in a way that sounds
like Paul is also working to forgive them.

Instead of wallowing in all those who've left him, Paul starts
gathering allies. He pulls those he knows he can trust in closer to
him and surrounds himself with people who will build him up. This
is so difficult in the moment! When we are miserable and alone,
there's a part of us that is convinced that it's best that way. If I had
my friends close by, I'd just make them miserable, too, so I should
just let them go on and be happy. Again, this is Satan's lie to keep
us alone.

We tend to read Hebrews 10:25 as a cudgel. It is the "You better
come to church; the Bible says so!" verse. There is truth in that application. The verse specifically says not to forsake the assembly.

That instruction doesn't exist in a vacuum, though. We are not
instructed to assemble just because God wants us to check that
item off our to-do list. There is a reason, a why, for the instruction
to assemble. God knows that we are our best selves when we are
surrounded with those who have a similar purpose. We think better, love better, and do better when we are in a group of those who
are thinking well, loving well, and doing good because of God.
When we are with our spiritual family, we are better able to shrug
off the weight of isolation and get to work as God has planned for
us.

Discussion Questions

1. How do we react to the words of Psalm 88? Do you feel like he's being overly dramatic? Have you ever felt as alone as the psalmist feels in that moment?

2. Where does isolation show up in your life? What lie is the devil telling you that keeps you isolated?

3. Telling someone they're not alone is fine, but is it enough? What else can we do to help those who feel isolated?

4. Who are your Demas, Crescens, and Titus? Who has abandoned you? What was your response in the moment when they abandoned you?

5. What is your why for assembling? What good works are you provoked to? What good works can you provoke in those around you?

Project 1

Make a list. Who are your people? Who are your fellow travelers? Who helps remind you that even when you feel alone, you're not? Don't be vague here. Write names! Pick one of those people and tell them how much it means to you to have them walking the path with you.

_____

_____

_____

_____

_____

_____

_____

_____

_____

_____

_____

_____

_____

Project 2

What connection do you see between hopelessness and isolation? How do they work together? Have you seen this in real life? Draw a diagram showing the interconnectedness of the two ideas.

_____

_____

_____

_____

_____

_____

_____

_____

_____

_____

_____

_____

_____

Lesson Twelve
Answering with Challenges

Read: Psalm 74.

Sing: Psalm 74, to the tune of "Where the Roses Never Fade."

Why, O Lord, have You rejected
Those You purchased with Your grace?
For the foe has conquered Zion
And defiled Your dwelling place.
In their hearts they chose to crush us,
And no prophet knows how long;
Will they spurn Your name forever?
Will You not destroy their wrong?

Yet of old You are my ruler;
You deliver by Your might;
When Leviathan opposed You,
You destroyed him in the fight.
You subdue both streams and torrents;
You control both night and day;
You set limits on creation,
And the seasons all obey.

Know, O Lord, the foe reviles You,
And the fools have spurned Your love;
Do not give us to the lions
Nor forget Your turtledove!
Rise and plead Your cause with justice;
Hear the fools who cry anew;
When they mock Your name, remember;
Constantly, they scoff at You.

React

What was your reaction to reading the psalm? _____

_____

_____

_____

_____

What was your reaction to singing the psalm? _____

_____

_____

_____

_____

Study

My 10-year-old son went to play at a friend's house for the day. My boy can be a little mouthy at times, but he's a good boy. He and his friend were playing video games together, and the friend's father was outside on the back deck. He called in for the boys to put the video games away and do something else for a while. My son immediately responded by asking why. This is pretty common in our house—our children want to know why we do everything! This is not common in his friend's house, though. Without missing a beat, his friend's father responded, "In this house, we don't ask why. In this house, we say yes sir!" My son and his friend jumped to shut off the video games and find something else to do!

Challenging God is such a dicey topic. We read stories in the Old Testament (and in the New Testament, for that matter) of God striking people dead, and we get nervous. Sometimes, God's punishments don't make sense to us, so we get nervous and decide we're going to play it safe. We worry that we're going to be met with a divine "We say yes sir!" if we question or challenge God at all, ever, about anything.

The Scripture is full of people challenging God, though! Psalm 74 is full of challenges to God. Asaph begins the psalm by asking, as the psalmists often do, why God has rejected His people, and how long He will continue to reject them. Even this feels a little concerning—if I truly think God has rejected me, I worry He might have a good reason for having done so!

From there, though, the Psalm gets even more explicit in challenging God. Asaph quickly moves from questions to statements. Now he's not asking God where He's gone; he's telling God to get back over here and do something. Okay, at this point I'm officially uncomfortable. I do not get to boss God around!

That's exactly what this psalmist does, though, and he's not alone. Many psalms have the Israelites reminding God of His promises (as though He's forgotten!) and telling Him that He needs to get on with fulfilling those promises. Can you even imagine? What would you think if a sister in Christ started praying this way at your next ladies' Bible study? What would you do if she started demanding in a public prayer that God show up and do what He said He would? That's exactly what this psalm is—a public prayer, though sung, that tells God that He promised not to forsake them, and so He better get down here. Myself, I'd be edging away from that sister during her prayer, so that the lightning didn't accidentally strike me, too!

We've had conversations on the other side of this, though, haven't we? I've had many a conversation with a sister who tells me that she feels like God has forgotten her. She struggles to pray anymore because she thinks God doesn't hear her. She sees others having their prayers answered, and she knows that God is good and delights in His people, just... not in her. She feels abandoned. Of course, I tell her she's not. I tell her to wait on the Lord, to be strong and take courage. I tell her to keep bringing her requests to God.

This ties in pretty directly with feelings of hopelessness and isolation. If things in our earthly life feel hopeless, yet we are the people of God, it's easy to feel like God is behind whatever's going wrong in our lives. We want to put our hope in God, but He hasn't done much to help us here, so we probably shouldn't put too much hope in Him. When we are lonely and isolated, it's easy to project that onto God as well. People here want nothing to do with me, no one likes me, so why would the God of the universe like me, either? He's got much better people to spend His time on.

All of that is why it's so important to be willing to challenge God. Of course, the key in Psalm 74, and the key for us, is to challenge Him on what He's actually said. It's one thing to remind God of the promises He made. It's another altogether to put words in God's mouth, assume promises He hasn't made, and then get upset with Him for not keeping the promise He didn't make! God hasn't promised me earthly happiness, in the general or specific. He hasn't promised me a husband, or a baby, or a great job, or a perfect house. He hasn't promised me lots of money, or a healthy body, or fabulous vacations. I don't get to challenge Him to keep those promises, because He didn't make them!

So, what do I get to challenge Him on? The things He has promised. He's promised heaven. He's promised a family of His people. He's promised consolation and comfort in the Holy Spirit. He's promised to be with me always! These things are worth so much more than great vacations or fulfilling careers. They're easy to overlook, though, because they're not tangible.

Gideon was made a promise, and he pretty immediately challenged God on it. Judges 6 tells the story of Gideon hearing that he will lead God's people. As they head into battle, Gideon asks God for a sign that he's on the right track. He gives God a very specific sign—a fleece wet with dew, and the ground around it dry. God performs the sign just as Gideon asks, and performs it abundantly, so that Gideon can wring water out of the fleece!

Gideon goes a step further, though. The next night, he asks God for another sign—with the preface, "Please don't be mad!" This time, he asks for the reverse—the fleece dry, and ground around it wet. Again, God performs the sign as asked. No thunderstorms of anger, no lightning strikes of retribution! We get nervous reading Gideon's story. I've heard it explained away so many times. Well, that was the Old Testament. Well, Gideon was special. Well, it was different when God talked to people directly. Well, the age of miraculous signs is over.

It was the Old Testament. Gideon was special. God did talk directly to people. The age of miraculous signs is over. However, God is the same. The same God who was willing to reassure Gideon of the promises that God had made is willing to reassure us as well! So long as we are willing to believe God, as Gideon was, God will reassure us in the face of our challenges.

Hebrews 4:14-16 reminds us that in Jesus, we have a High Priest who understands us. He gets it. In a visceral way that God the Father does not, Jesus gets what it is to be a human and to experience life and temptation.

He went through all of that without sinning, but He didn't do that so that He could go back to heaven and look down His nose at us and gripe about our inability to do what needs to be done. Instead, He walked on this world so that He could go back and advocate for us, so that He could grant us access. We have access to come boldly before God's throne and make our needs known! As opposed to Esther, who went into the throne room of the king with nervousness and timidity, we go boldly into our King's throne room, because Jesus paved the way for us to do so!

Psalms on Anxiety and Depression

Discussion Questions

1. What feelings do you have about Asaph's conversation with God in Psalm 74? Are you comfortable with the way he's talking to God?

2. What should we tell people who feel like God isn't listening?

3. What are some promises God has made to you?

4. How do we feel about asking for signs as Gideon did? Are our feelings informed by Scripture? Why or why not?

5. What does Jesus understand about you in particular? What part of His human experience resonates with you?

Project 1

Make a chart of the promises that God has made, and how He's kept them. Share your chart with your sisters and see if anyone else's chart contains things that remind you of other ways God has kept His promises!

Project 2

Go boldly! Find a promise that God has made that speaks to your heart and your needs right now and pray it boldly. Remind God of the promises He's made and hold Him to it! Pray His promises and let Him reassure you that He will fulfill them!

Psalms on Anxiety and Depression

Lesson Thirteen

Review

Read: Psalm 42.

Sing: Psalm 42, to the tune of "When My Love to Christ Grows Weak."

Thirsting for the living God,
Seeking favor in His sight,
Still I feed upon my tears
While I sorrow day and night.

In my grief, I call to mind
How I worshiped with the throng,
Coming to the house of God,
Joining there in joyful song.

Why are you cast down, my soul?
Why are you disturbed within?
Put your confidence in God;
I will praise Him once again.

As I mourn I think of God
Though I struggle in the deep;
He commands His love by day,
And His song will bless my sleep.

I exclaim to God my rock,
"Why have You forgotten me?"
I am wounded in my bones,
Daily faced with mockery.

Why are you cast down, my soul?
Why are you disturbed within?
Put your confidence in God;
I will praise Him once again.

React

What was your reaction to reading the psalm? _____

_____

_____

_____

_____

What was your reaction to singing the psalm? _____

_____

_____

_____

_____

Study

Anxiety and depression, and mental illness more generally, are incredibly complex and difficult topics. They're even more difficult to live through! One of the most difficult parts of anxiety and depression is the way they warp our thinking to make it more difficult to escape them. Thankfully, God's word hasn't left us without a toolbox to deal with this problem.

In order to use that toolbox, though, we have to acknowledge its presence. It is a great temptation to only engage in hymn worship that fits our cultural expectations. The ideal Christian should be happy all the time, we think, and only ever praise God and thank Him for His good provisions, and so that's what our hymns should look like. We veer toward hymns that fit that mold, and sing only peppy, uplifting hymns. Even when we turn to the psalms, we cherry-pick the cheery psalms, or the cheery phrases out of otherwise not-cheery psalms. We sing the happy and leave the rest buried in the Old Testament somewhere.

Because of this tendency, our emotional expression in modern worship is stunted. What do we do when there is a great tragedy? What do we do when a beloved family member has been called to their reward, and we're bereft without them? What do we do when we're mired in anxiety and depression and don't see a way out? We don't sing, that's for sure, because we don't have hymns that deal with those emotions.

The toolbox of the Psalms, on the other hand, gives us a fantastic range of emotions to sing. If you're happy and everything's great, there's a psalm for that. If you're miserably sad, there's a psalm for that. If you're feeling utterly alone and hopeless, there's a psalm for that. Angry? Abandoned by God? Confused about what to do next? Yep. Psalms for those, too. God has given us such a depth of emotional expression in the Psalms, and we ignore that at our peril.

Psalms on Anxiety and Depression

If you are reading this and struggling through anxiety, depression, or some other mental illness, know that you do not have to do this alone. Seek professional help, for sure. The assistance of a doctor and a therapist are invaluable in dealing with mental health, just as they are in dealing with physical health. But know, too, that God has not left you alone in this. Whatever you're struggling with, there is consolation and fellowship in the psalms to show you God's way through the pain of this life.

Discussion Questions

1. What does the book of Psalms teach us about physical health and mental illness?

2. How does authenticity give us a tool to combat mental illness?

3. What does the book of Psalms teach us about the lack of a happy ending?

4. How does meditation give us a tool to combat mental illness?

5. What does the book of Psalms teach us about waiting and uncertainty?

6. How does repetition give us a tool to combat mental illness?

7. What does the book of Psalms teach us about sin and mental illness?

8. How does speaking truth give us a tool to combat mental illness?

9. What does the book of Psalms teach us about hopelessness?

10. What does the book of Psalms teach us about isolation?

11. How do challenges give us a tool to combat mental illness?

12. What have you learned about mental health from this study?

THE PSALMS USED IN THIS BOOK ARE FROM

Worshiping with the

℘salms

By M.W. Bassford

Worshiping with the
Psalms
978-158427-544-2

Worshiping with the
Psalms: Companion Text
978-158427-545-9

Worshiping with the
Psalms: PowerPoint
978-158427-544-2PPT

ORDER FROM:

Truth Publications, Inc.
CEI Bookstore
220 S. Marion St., Athens, AL 35611
855-492-6657
sales@truthpublications.com
www.truthbooks.com